To Beth - m[y] ["] friend" -
love, Kim

MY FRIEND, YOU'VE BEEN AN
Angel

PAINTINGS BY
Susan Winget

HARVEST HOUSE PUBLISHERS

EUGENE, OREGON

The road to a friend's house is never long.

DANISH PROVERB

My Friend, You've Been an Angel
Copyright © 2006 by Harvest House Publishers
Eugene, Oregon 97402

ISBN–13: 978-0-7369-1795-7
ISBN–10: 0-7369-1795-0

The artwork of Susan Winget © 2006 is used by Harvest House Publishers, Inc. under authorization from Courtney Davis, Inc. For more information regarding art prints featured in this book, please contact:

    Courtney Davis, Inc.
    55 Francisco Street, Suite 450
    San Francisco, CA 94133
    www.susanwinget.com

Design and production by Koechel Peterson & Associates, Inc., Minneapolis, Minnesota

$\mathcal{M}$iss Barry was a kindred spirit, after all,"
Anne confided to Marilla. "You wouldn't think
so to look at her, but she is. You don't find it
right out at first, as in Matthew's case, but after
a while you come to see it. Kindred spirits are not
so scarce as I used to think. It's splendid to find
out there are so many of them in the world."

L.M. MONTGOMERY

Anne of Green Gables

Breathless, we flung us
on the windy hill,
Laughed in the sun,
and kissed the lovely grass.

RUPERT BROOKE

WE TAKE CARE OF OUR HEALTH,
WE LAY UP MONEY, WE MAKE
OUR ROOF TIGHT AND OUR
CLOTHING SUFFICIENT,
BUT WHO PROVIDES WISELY
THAT HE SHALL NOT BE
WANTING THE BEST PROPERTY
OF ALL—FRIENDS?

Ralph Waldo Emerson

I am speaking now of
the highest duty we owe our friends,
the noblest, the most sacred—
that of keeping their own nobleness,
goodness, pure and incorrupt.

HARRIET·BEECHER·STOWE

Prayer is the rustling of the wings of the angels
who are bringing the blessing to us.
Charles Spurgeon

O who will walk a mile with me
   Along life's merry way?
A comrade blithe and full of glee,
Who dares to laugh out loud and free,
And let his frolic fancy play,
Like a happy child, through the flowers gay
That fill the field and fringe the way
Where he walks a mile with me.

And who will walk a mile with me
Along life's weary way?
A friend whose heart has eyes to see
The stars shine out o'er the darkening lea,
And the quiet rest at the end o' the day,—
A friend who knows, and dares to say,
The brave, sweet words that cheer the way
Where he walks a mile with me.

With such a comrade, such a friend,
I fain would walk till journey's end,
Through summer sunshine, winter rain,
And then?—Farewell, we shall meet again!

HENRY VAN DYKE

When you least expect it, a common thread—golden,
at that—begins to weave together the fabric of friendship.

Mary Kay Shanley

A home-made friend wears longer than one you buy in the market.

Austin O'Malley

Friends are the thermometer by which
we may judge the temperature
of our fortunes.

LADY MARGUERITE BLESSINGTON

It's what each of us sows, and how,

that gives to us character and prestige.

Seeds of kindness, goodwill, and

human understanding, planted in

fertile soil, spring up into deathless

friendships, big deeds of worth, and

a memory that will not soon fade...

GEORGE MATTHEW ADAMS

Everywhere Ruth was,

that's where Idgie would be.

It was a mutual thing.

They just took to each other,

and you could hear them,

sittin' on the swing on the porch,

gigglin' all night.

FANNIE FLAGG

Fried Green Tomatoes at the
Whistle Stop Café

AT LAST THE TIME FOR MY GOING CAME. I was to leave the next day. Someone I knew gave a party in my honour, to which all the village was invited. It was midwinter; there was nothing in the gardens but a few dahlias and chrysanthemums, and I suppose that for two hundred miles round there was not a rose to be bought for love or money. Only in the garden of a friend of mine, in a sunny corner between the oven and the brick wall, there was a rose tree growing which had on it one bud. It was white, and it had been promised to the fair-haired girl to wear at the party.

The evening came; when I arrived and went to the waiting-room, to take off my mantle, I found the girl there already. She was dressed in pure white, with her great white arms and shoulders showing, and her bright hair glittering in the candle-light, and the white rose fastened at her breast. She looked like a queen. I said, "Good evening," and turned away quickly to the glass to arrange my old black scarf across my old black dress.

Then I felt a hand touch my hair.

"Stand still," she said.

I looked in the glass. She had taken the white rose from her breast, and was fastening it in my hair.

"How nice dark hair is; it sets off flowers so." She stepped back and looked at me. "It looks much better there!"

I turned around.

"You are so beautiful to me," I said.

"Y-e-s," she said, with her slow Colonial drawl; "I'm so glad."

We stood looking at each other. Then they came in and swept us away to dance. All the evening we did not come near to each other. Only once, as she passed, she smiled at me.

The next morning I left the town. I never saw her again.

Years afterwards I heard she had married and gone to America; it may or may not be so—but the rose—the rose is in the box still! When my faith in woman grows dim, and it seems that for want of love and magnaminity she can play no part in any future heaven; then the scent of that small withered thing comes back:—spring cannot fail us.

OLIVE SCHREINER
The Woman's Rose

MISS TAYLOR MARRIED. It was Miss Taylor's loss which first brought grief. It was on the wedding-day of this beloved friend that Emma first sat in mournful thought of any continuance…The want of Miss Taylor would be felt every hour of every day…She had been a friend and companion such as few possessed, intelligent, well-informed, useful, gentle, knowing all the ways of the family, interested in all its concerns, and peculiarly interested in herself, in every pleasure, every scheme of hers—one to whom she could speak every thought as it arose, and who had such an affection for her as could never find fault.

JANE AUSTEN
Emma

When any of us needs a loving heart or a helping hand, it's our friends we turn to, and the very acts of loving and helping in turn help cement our friendships. In fact, the relationships that last and grow over the years are often the ones that have been tested in the crucible of need.

EMILIE BARNES

My only sketch; profile of Heaven
is a large blue sky, and larger than the
biggest I have seen in June—
and in it are my friends—every one of them.

EMILY DICKINSON

I have learned that to have a good friend is the purest of all God's gifts, for it is a love that has no exchange of payment.

Frances Farmer

The angels are the dispensers and

administrators of the Divine beneficence

toward us; they regard our safety,

undertake our defense, direct our ways,

and exercise a constant solicitude

that no evil befall us.

JOHN CALVIN

WE DROVE TO MEEKATHARRA…to pick up Jen and Toly…I couldn't speak when I first saw them, but I held on to them tight. Seeing them and touching them was like a dose of tonic. They understood. They stroked my ruffled feathers and forced me to laugh.

ROBYN DAVIDSON
Tracks

There are friends, I think, we can't imagine living without. People who are sisters to us, or brothers.

JULIE REECE DEAVER

15

A Friend or Two

There's all of pleasure and all of peace
In a friend or two;
And all your troubles may find release
Within a friend or two;
It's in the grip of the sleeping hand
On native soil or in alien land,
But the world is made—
   do you understand—
Of a friend or two.

A song to sing, and a crust to share
With a friend or two;
A smile to give and a grief to bear
With a friend or two;
A road to walk and a goal to win,
An inglenook to find comfort in,
The gladdest hours that we know begin
With a friend or two.

A little laughter, perhaps some tears
With a friend or two;
The days, the weeks, and the months
   and years
With a friend or two;

A vale to cross and a hill to climb,
A mock at age and a jeer at time—
The prose of life takes the lilt of rhyme
With a friend or two.

The brother-soul and the brother-heart
Of a friend or two
Make us drift on from the crowd apart,
With a friend or two;
For come days happy or come days sad
We count no hours but the ones made glad
By the hale good times we have ever had
With a friend or two.

Then brim the goblet and quaff the toast
To a friend or two,
For glad the man who can always boast
Of a friend or two;
But fairest sight is a friendly face,
The blithest tread is a friendly pace,
And heaven will be a better place
For a friend or two.

WILBUR D. NESBIT

THE HUGE LION MOVED slowly, moaning in pain: There was a thorn in his paw. Androcles forgot his fear and quickly helped the lion by removing the thorn from his paw. The lion gratefully licked Androcles' face, and a most unusual friendship was born.

AESOP

I believe that we are always attracted to what we need most, an instinct leading us toward the persons who are to open new vistas in our lives and fill them with new knowledge.

HELENE ISWOLSKI

I do not wish to treat friendships daintily,

but with roughest courage. When they are real,

they are not glass threads or frostwork,

but the solidest thing we know.

RALPH WALDO EMERSON

Silences make the real conversations between friends.
Not the saying but the never needing to say is what counts.

Margaret Lee Runbeck

No love, no friendship can cross the path of our destiny without leaving some mark on it forever.

FRANÇOIS MAURIAC

OUR FRIENDS INTERPRET THE WORLD
AND OURSELVES TO US, IF WE TAKE THEM
TENDERLY AND TRULY.

Amos Bronson Alcott

He who sows courtesy reaps friendship, and he who plants kindness gathers love.

SAINT BASIL

The rain may be falling hard outside,
But your smile makes it all alright.
I'm so glad that you're my friend.
I know our friendship will never end.

ROBERT ALAN

*Friends are as companions on a journey,
who ought to aid each other to persevere
in the road to a happier life.*

Pythagoras

My friends have made the story of my life. In a thousand ways they have turned my limitations into beautiful privileges, and enabled me to walk serene and happy in the shadow cast by my deprivation.

HELEN KELLER

I suppose there is one friend in the life of each of us who seems not a separate person, however dear and beloved, but an expansion, an interpretation, of one's self, the very meaning of one's soul.

EDITH WHARTON

We've been long together...through pleasant and through cloudy weather.

ANNA LAETITIA BARBAULD

GOD DOESN'T SEND THEM BECAUSE WE DESERVE IT. HE SENDS THEM BECAUSE WE NEED HELP. ANGELS ARE LITERALLY MESSENGERS OF GOD'S MERCY.

Mac Hammond

*In real friendship
the judgment, the
genius, the prudence
of each party become
the common
property of both.*

Maria Edgeworth

Trouble is a sieve through which we sift our acquaintances.
Those too big to pass through are our friends.

Arlene Francis

There are people whom one loves immediately and forever. Even to know they are alive in the world with one is quite enough.

NANCY SPAIN

The responsibilities of friendship? To talk. And to listen.

ROSIE THOMAS

SO LONG AS WE SERVE; SO LONG AS WE ARE LOVED BY OTHERS, I WOULD ALMOST SAY THAT WE ARE INDISPENSABLE.

Robert Louis Stevenson

THE FRIENDSHIP WAS FIRMLY cemented. It had a rock-hard basis called shared experience, or the tolerance developed from seeing someone at their best and at their worst, and stripped of all social value—the bare bones of another human being.

ROBYN DAVIDSON
Tracks

For he shall give his angels charge over thee . . . to keep thee in all thy ways

Psalm 91:11

A friend loveth at all times.

To know someone here or there with whom you can feel
there is understanding in spite of distances or thoughts expressed—
that can make life a garden.

GOETHE

The making of
friends, who are real
friends, is the best
token we have of a
man's success in life.

EDWARD EVERETT
HALE

There comes that
mysterious meeting in
life when someone
acknowledges who we are
and what we can be,
igniting the circuits of
our highest potential.

Rusty Berkus

New Friends & Old Friends

Make new friends, but keep the old;
Those are silver, these are gold.
New-made friendships, like new wine,
Age will mellow and refine.
Friendships that have stood the test—
Time and change—are surely best;
Brow may wrinkle, hair grow gray,
Friendship never knows decay.
For 'mid old friends, tried and true,
Once more we our youth renew.
But old friends, alas! may die,
New friends must their place supply.
Cherish friendship in your breast—
New is good, but old is best;
Make new friends, but keep the old;
Those are silver, these are gold.

JOSEPH PARRY

I my Companions see
In you, another Me.

Thomas Traherne

Friendship that flows from the heart cannot be frozen by adversity, as the water that flows from the spring cannot congeal in winter.

JAMES FENNIMORE COOPER

Friendship, peculiar boon of Heav'n,
The noble mind's delight and pride,
To men and angels only giv'n…

SAMUEL JOHNSON

THE MOST I CAN DO for my friend is simply to be his friend. I have no wealth to bestow on him. If he knows that I am happy in loving him, he will want no other reward. Is not friendship divine in this?

HENRY DAVID THOREAU

Friendship without self-interest is one of the rare and beautiful things in life.

James Francis Byrnes

I'd like to be the sort of friend that you have been to me;

I'd like to be the help that you've been always glad to be;

I'd like to mean as much to you each minute of the day
As you have meant, old friend of mine,
to me along the way.

I'm wishing at this time
that I could but repay
A portion of the gladness that
you've strewn along my way;

And could I have one wish
this year,
this only would it be:
I'd like to be the
sort of friend that
you have been to me.

EDGAR A. GUEST